With Your Latte

With Your Latte

A Little Wisdom to Lighten Your Way

Charles R. Ringma

RESOURCE *Publications* • Eugene, Oregon

WITH YOUR LATTE
A Little Wisdom to Lighten Your Way

Copyright © 2020 Charles R. Ringma. All rights reserved. Except for brief quotations in critical publications or reviews, no part of this book may be reproduced in any manner without prior written permission from the publisher. Write: Permissions, Wipf and Stock Publishers, 199 W. 8th Ave., Suite 3, Eugene, OR 97401.

Resource Publications
An Imprint of Wipf and Stock Publishers
199 W. 8th Ave., Suite 3
Eugene, OR 97401

www.wipfandstock.com

PAPERBACK ISBN: 978-1-7252-7312-2
HARDCOVER ISBN: 978-1-7252-7313-9
EBOOK ISBN: 978-1-7252-7314-6

Manufactured in the U.S.A.   06/11/20

Preface

WE LIVE IN A world of sound bites. Many are frivolous, reactive, and don't say all that much. Some may stop us in our tracks and momentarily catch our attention. Some may call us to deeper reflection. I hope this little book will do this while you are enjoying your morning coffee or riding on the train or bus to work.

Sound-bite wisdom may sound a little odd. Can a couple of brief lines really say something meaningful? Don't we need more complicated philosophical or ethical systems to make sense of life? Maybe we do! But since so many of us claim to be time poor and can only give a few minutes to the task of becoming more mindful, we may have to settle for some sound-bite wisdom. So give it try—not just to *read* one page, but to *sit* with it for some time. Don't let your coffee get cold!

At this point in the twenty-first century we don't need more diversion and escapism, but we do need to become more thoughtful, reflective, and proactive. There is much to celebrate and much about which we should be concerned. We need a renewed focus on what is important for a sustainable and good life on planet earth, which is a wounded creature doing its best to sustain us.

Not only should this cause us deep concern and committed action, but we also need to create a more caring humanity, one marked by friendship and respect rather than suspicion and exclusion.

In addition to these big challenges, there are many other things to think about that have to do with meaning, purpose, and human flourishing. Goodness—it's enough to make you want to order a second coffee!

This reflective reader holds no major theories or philosophical, religious, or ethical systems—only sound bites. There is nothing strident in these pages—just gentle nudges. Maybe a fragile wisdom is not born in our

Preface

prowess, rationality, and pragmatism. Instead, maybe it is born in places of unknowing, seeking, longing, and crying?

So welcome to this little book, which will sit nicely alongside your cup of coffee. Digest these sound bites at your leisure.

My thanks, first and foremost, to all who have enriched my life, including members of my extended family, the "holy scribblers,"[1] and the people with whom I have worked in Brisbane, Manila, Yangon, and Vancouver. And thanks to Patrick-Charles McLaren, Maryanne Hughes, and Karen Hollenbeck-Wuest who have given valuable feedback.

Charles Ringma,
Brisbane, Australia
2020

---

1. The scribblers, a writer's group that meets for writer's retreats and a weekly day of writing, include: Irene Alexander, Chris Brown, Terry Gatfield, Jill Manton, Tim McCowan, Ross McKenzie, Sarah Nicholls and Charles Ringma. You may connect with us on https://holyscribblers.blogspot.com

Introduction

IN LIFE'S JOURNEY WE all need a little help along the way. This is no affront to our dignity, nor our ability.

We can see something of the help we need from our therapeutic culture. So many of us have a life coach, counsellor, mentor, fitness trainer, therapist, yoga teacher, psychologist, or spiritual director, among others who offer us assistance.

More basically, we all gain support from our family, friends, colleagues, and neighbours.

Undergirding these supports are the institutions and resources in our society that help to make life more liveable and sustainable.

Most fundamentally, there is planet earth, which continues to give with such flagrant generosity, though we have exploited and wounded it so uncaringly and mercilessly.

As we are supported by all these good resources, we also need to make *our way* in life with meaning and purpose. So we make choices. We develop our values. We have our ideals. And in the fray of life, we seek to live well with generosity and fairness.

Of course, we face difficulties and disappointments along the way. Sometimes we feel that we have hit a brick wall and become wounded and "bloodied."

Thus life is forged in the midst of all that is given and also in what thwarts and robs us.

This reality calls us to deeper reflection, which helps us to embrace ambiguity, cry in our pain, and forgive, while it also empowers us to rage against injustice.

Maybe we all need a little *latte* wisdom to guide us as we face these and many other vulnerable issues and challenges.

Introduction

As you read each sound bite of *latte* wisdom, you may wish to scribble a response to the following questions: *What larger issues are at play? What is the invitation for me? How should I respond?*

May this small book befriend you!

The more firmly we cling to our iron-clad certainties,
the more life's questions
will shrivel,
and our "world" will become diminished and irrelevant.

Of course, we need some certainties.
We need ground under our feet.
But these certainties must grow out of faith, hope, and love,
and they must serve the common good
rather than our narrow concerns and insecurities.

There are certainties based on facts,
but many are based on personal conviction.
Thus we claim to be sure that *this* is how we should live,
and *this* is what we should do.
Such certainties can be precious gifts, but they need to be
reflected in the mirror of kindness and justice for all.

The most difficult choices
are often not
between good and bad,
but between one good and another.

We can't be and do anything and everything.
We need to embrace human limitation
and our particularity in time and place.

Plant a tree—
and show that life is not only about me!

When St. Francis, the rich romantic and swashbuckling mercenary,
kissed the leper,
he showed that a strange event
can be the place of personal transformation.

While we may long for priestly oil
to salve our guilty conscience,
we need prophetic insight and courage
to bring us on the road to justice.

When you have finally succeeded,
having made mistakes
along the way,
be generous
in allowing others to make and learn
from their mistakes.

While we should make important
life-directional choices,
sometimes unexpected circumstances
open a doorway
that we may walk through.

An army may be stoppable.
The forces of nature are not.
Nor can one stop the flow of new ideas
that seek to solve our ecological and other crises.

To be tough-minded
and
tenderhearted
is a rare,
but beautiful, way
of being in the world.

The obvious difference between an open hand and a closed fist is not simply the difference between vulnerability and violence, but also between receptivity and rejection.

Life is not simply about self-determination,
but also about responding to unexpected things
that come our way.

Our *wants* are often so long.
Our *needs* are shorter
and should be governed by the needs of others.

The saying, "think globally, act locally,"
needs to be complemented with,
"act globally to salvage what is local."

We all have some power and human agency—
no matter how small its potency and reach—
but it must be used *for* and on *behalf of* others,
not simply *over* others and for ourselves.

Self-care need not be at enmity
with the practice of hospitality.

The myth of self-sufficiency
puts us in ever greater danger of manipulation
by those who seek to exploit
our unacknowledged needs.

In the modern world
of fragile and vulnerable families
and large institutional configurations of power,
we need to build intermediate structures
of friendship and solidarity.

The act of giving
cannot simply come from abundance.
It comes, first and foremost,
from a generous heart.

Questions arise when the smooth seas
of our lives
are unexpectedly disturbed.

To be dislocated
does not leave us in an empty space,
but in a *liminal* place,
where the unexpected might emerge.

To need help
does not affront our dignity,
but simply acknowledges
our human condition.

Tradition may well seem outmoded, stale, and irrelevant.
Our first move is often to abandon it,
but creatively reappropriating it may be more viable.

Hesitate before you jump.
Second thoughts are not a sign of weakness.

If you don't fear silence,
it
can both disarm and nurture you.

If *we* have lost *our* way,
who or what can bring us home?

Home is not only our private dwelling,
but also our neighbourhood
and the earth itself.

Friendship is not merely association,
but the place where heart matters
truly matter.

Crying may not be a sign of weakness,
but rather the assertion of life
in the face of great distress.

The courage to act
comes
from the courage to be
who you are meant to be
and do what you are called to do.

Be courageous,
but don't be impetuous, rash, or foolhardy.

Life, as much as school, is the great educator, though we may learn its lessons more slowly.

Don't waste your sorrows,
and don't squander your successes or victories.

When all seems lost, allow yourself to fall.
You may rise again in unexpected ways.

When a major phase in your life comes to an end,
don't be afraid
to let your hands lie idle for a time.

If you decide to abandon your traditional gods,
make sure
that the gods of your own making
are more benign.

We have taken and taken.
The earth is exhausted and wounded.
It is time to give back.
We will *all* need to make sacrifices.

From the places of marginality,
one can see things
that others often cannot imagine.

Make sure that whomever you follow
has a limp like Jacob,
who wrestled with an angel in the night,
was broken, and then renewed.

We are both wounded healers
and those in need
of healing.

The greatest gift that we can receive
from another person
is the freedom to be ourselves.

While we may long for the tranquil waters
of the lagoon,
we will soon become bored
and seek life's challenges in stormy seas.

While our own achievements tend to take
centre stage,
the cast of any life
is comprised of what we have been given by others
rather than our solo performances.

While long-term dependency
is an unhealthy state of affairs,
receptivity
is a sign of maturity.

When we live the myth of the self
as a constant self-creation,
we embrace a most wearisome burden.

Willing and doing are core features
of being human,
but so are dreaming,
visioning,
and matters of the heart.

When we are *a part of* existing institutions—
and *apart from* them
at the same time—
we live a healthy, but challenging, dialectic.

To withhold utter loyalties
may well safeguard
the sacredness of our inner being.

When the delicate membranes
of our inner being
have been violated by abuse and betrayal,
we become capable
of perpetrating the greatest evil.

Is your social self,
which is so fragrantly displayed in all your social settings,
undergirded by an inner self
of integrity and virtue?

Our marketeers understand
that we are not only geared to much-having
but to significance.
Thus it's all about image—
a god-like quality, indeed!

If you have never had to ask
for forgiveness,
you lack self-insight
and need to find your proper place in the human community.

When you deliberately seek to be
in a place of stillness,
you may gain the gift of solitude,
which will nurture
your inner being.

We don't always need advice,
but we do need lots of
encouragement.

We are amazingly complex creatures
and are often a mystery
even to ourselves.
Don't try to undo this mystery.
We are not machines.

We are never fully fulfilled,
and so we live with a *longing* heart.
Don't try to fill it.
Keep it empty.

We may be able to bring about a little change,
but most change
happens due to external factors.
The change we need to embrace, suffer, or resist
calls for the utmost discernment.

The greatest gift we can give ourselves
is not many things,
but the gentle assurance that even though
we do not always succeed,
we have done our best.

Life will wound us.
We all experience misunderstanding,
rejection,
and betrayal.
But this wounding need not destroy us.
for it can make us
resilient and determined
not to hurt others in the same way.

Our society and culture
constantly tell us that our hands need to be full,
but when our hands are empty,
we can receive new gifts.

Western culture has long celebrated
the solo hero,
but friendship-makers and
community-builders
make life sustainable.

Every social institution has its
strengths and weaknesses.
Thus we are all called to the
priestly task of maintenance
and the prophetic task of transformation.

Life is not one single event,
no matter how good or bad,
but rather a mosaic
of choices and commitments,
no matter how easy or difficult.

We don't always grasp the nettle,
and so an opportunity readily slips out of our hand.
This is not the end.
New possibilities come our way, and we will be
wiser for having failed the first time.

By all means, pursue
singular or multiple career paths,
but somewhere
along the way,
discover your *vocation*,
who you are truly meant to be and
what you are truly meant to do.

Hope is not only some
euphoric feeling for a better future,
but a painful and probing anticipation
of what can yet be.

Our pathway
may well be strewn with disappointments,
but resilience
is not forged through picnics.

This has taken so long,
because I did not take the time
to make it shorter.

A great loneliness
is to be ahead of your time.

The icicles of doubt, fear, and disappointment
can readily numb
the membranes of the heart,
but living with gratitude and wonder
keeps the heart tender.

We would all like
a better, fairer, and more peaceful world.
One small step
in this direction
is *to be* the change we would like *to see*.

Sometimes we overreach.
We try to do too much.
The task is beyond us.
This failure
is but a steppingstone
to try again
in a different way.

Joy
can only bubble to the surface
from wells of
wonder, simplicity,
and gratitude.

Don't overcalculate!
You may freeze yourself into inactivity.
Life is about risk-taking.
Even love takes risks.

We all need to be saved
from something
so that we may live purposively
for something.

If you are deeply concerned about something,
let your voice be heard.
A voice of truth
will find resonance with others.
It will also encounter resistance
and be an invitation to suffering.

When we erode
the delicate fabric
of community,
bureaucratic structures
have to provide
the framework for our lives.

Our life journey
is comprised
of distinct phases
that do not drop off like a rocket,
but continue.
The challenge, therefore, is to make sure
that the first phase
can sustain and nurture the other phases.

Of course, we desire and look for
love.
But when love finds us,
we marvel at the
magnificence of life.

At the time of
unrequited love,
we feel like a monumental failure.
One year later,
our wailing may seem like a small whimper.

Allow some more days to pass,
and the pressing matter—
while in no way less important—
may seem more manageable.

Physical poverty
is a blight on our humanity.
Poverty of
spirit
and hope
diminishes all of us.

For the monks
in silent prayer at 4 am,
the space between heaven and earth
is invitingly small.

The quickest path
may be
circuitous.

If others
carry the goodness
we have passed on to them,
then we have defied
the banality and finality of death.

If paradox
can dynamite rationalism,
then imagination
can trump paradox.

If you have never made an
enemy,
then you have never
said or done anything of
significance.

Dogged dogmatism
is not solved by
porous relativism,
but by forming communities
of conversation and dialogue.

If theft and murder
do not break normative social values
and everything is relative,
then we will end up living
by the tyranny of the powerful.

While we would like our hands
to be clean,
we are all complicit in the
wrongdoing of our institutions
and society.

No matter how much we may try to forget
or rationalize
the wounding of peoples and cultures
in the colonial period,
it will go on haunting us
in the present.

Dreams
are an irruption
within our inner being.
Guard them with care and discernment!

We are not just passengers on
spaceship earth.[1]
We are participants, for good or ill,
in nature's well-being.

---

1. An amended quote from R. Buckminster Fuller in *Brewer's Famous Quotations*, ed. Nigel Rees (London: Weidenfeld & Nicolson, 2006), 205.

The final melody line
is not to live in balance,
though the Benedictine monks thought it was.
Rather, life needs radical proponents,
whose very lopsided passions
may heal our world.

In a dark world,
the poet and the artist may be
the first
to light a candle.

It's when we start to ask
probing questions
that new possibilities swim into view.

When one makes a
mistake,
it is best to acknowledge it
and then seek to repair it.
Mending is a most important task
in our social existence.

In the crowded traffic of a city,
we have to yield
to allow others into our lane.
Giving way to others
is as much a part of the fabric of life
as self-assertion.

Let the stillness
before sunrise
penetrate your inner being.
Allow the dusk
at day's end
help you lay down the labours of your day.

What we truly mourn
when lost,
is what we have deeply loved.

After the revolutionaries
come
the bureaucrats.

Existentially
we long for freedom.
But we don't live freedom well
and soon tie ourselves
in knots again.

A great loss
is to lose ourselves
in the midst
of much-doing.

Emancipation
is not only a social condition.
It is the dawning recognition
that the narrative
of those in power
no longer holds sway in my life.

Go to the desert!
It is not empty,
but filled with stillness
that may absorb
your over-anxious mind.

"From the tree of silence
hangs
the fruit of tranquillity."[1]
And this fruit
is the sacrament
of peacemaking and community building.

---

1. Quoted in Charles Ringma. *Chase Two Horses: Proverbs and Sayings for an Everyday Spirituality.* Manchester, UK, 2018, 140.

About the Author

CHARLES RINGMA IS A Dutch-born Australian. He has worked in Indigenous communities, with drug-addicted young people, and among the urban poor. He has also taught in tertiary institutions in Australia, Southeast Asia, and Canada. He is a Franciscan Tertiary, plants rainforest trees, is enamoured with his chickens, and writes books on spirituality. And yes, he has a PhD in philosophical hermeneutics. Visit charlesringma.com

www.ingramcontent.com/pod-product-compliance
Lightning Source LLC
LaVergne TN
LVHW020059090426
835510LV00040B/2447